TWEETABLE

BENJAMIN FRANKLIN

Infotainment Press

TWEETABLE

BENJAMIN FRANKLIN

QUIPS, QUOTES & OTHER ONE-LINERS

*A*n investment in knowledge pays the best interest.

❧

*T*he U. S. Constitution doesn't guarantee happiness, only the pursuit of it. You have to catch up with it yourself.

❧

*L*ife's tragedy is that we get old too soon and wise too late.

❧

*W*ine is constant proof that God loves us and loves to see us happy.

❧

*I*nstead of cursing the darkness, light a candle.

*A*ny fool can criticize, condemn and complain—and most fools do.

❧

*T*ell me and I forget. Teach me and I remember. Involve me and I learn.

❧

*T*hree can keep a secret, if two of them are dead.

❧

*W*ell done is better than well said.

❧

*H*e that is good for making excuses is seldom good for anything else.

*E*ither write something worth reading or do something worth writing.

❧

*H*onesty is the best policy.

❧

*L*ost time is never found again.

❧

*D*o not fear mistakes. You will know failure. Continue to reach out.

❧

*H*e that would live in peace and at ease must not speak all he knows or all he sees.

*G*uests, like fish, begin to smell after three days.

※

A good conscience is a continual Christmas.

※

*R*ebellion against tyrants is obedience to God.

※

*W*hatever is begun in anger ends in shame.

※

*W*ise men don't need advice. Fools won't take it.

*H*alf a truth is often a great lie.

*S*ome people die at 25 and aren't buried until 75.

*H*e that can have patience can have what he will.

A place for everything, everything in its place.

*B*eing ignorant is not so much a shame, as being unwilling to learn.

*I*n this world nothing can be said to be certain, except death and taxes.

☙

*W*e must, indeed, all hang together or, most assuredly, we shall all hang separately.

☙

A man wrapped up in himself makes a very small bundle.

☙

*Y*ou may delay, but time will not.

☙

*E*nergy and persistence conquer all things.

*W*ords may show a man's wit but actions his meaning.

❧

*B*e slow in choosing a friend, slower in changing.

❧

*E*ven peace may be purchased at too high a price.

❧

*T*ime is money.

❧

*C*ontent makes poor men rich; discontent makes rich men poor.

A penny saved is a penny earned.

࿇

*K*eep your eyes wide open before marriage, half shut afterwards.

࿇

I didn't fail the test, I just found 100 ways to do it wrong.

࿇

*D*istrust and caution are the parents of security.

࿇

*W*hen in doubt, don't.

*B*etter is a little with content
than much with contention.

She laughs at everything you say. Why? Because she has fine teeth.

※

Never leave that till tomorrow which you can do today.

※

Beware of little expenses. A small leak will sink a great ship.

※

If you would be loved, love, and be loveable.

※

If passion drives you, let reason hold the reins.

*A*nger is never without a reason, but seldom with a good one.

*T*here are three things extremely hard: steel, a diamond, and to know one's self.

*T*here was never a good war, or a bad peace.

*D*iligence is the mother of good luck.

*A*ll wars are follies, very expensive and very mischievous ones.

To succeed, jump as quickly at opportunities as you do at conclusions.

જ્જ

Take time for all things: great haste makes great waste.

જ્જ

The doors of wisdom are never shut.

જ્જ

Where there's marriage without love, there will be love without marriage.

જ્જ

God helps those who help themselves.

*S*peak ill of no man, but speak all the good you know of everybody.

❧

I saw few die of hunger; of eating, a hundred thousand.

❧

*H*e that lives upon hope will die fasting.

❧

*A*dmiration is the daughter of ignorance.

❧

*H*aving been poor is no shame, but being ashamed of it, is.

*W*here liberty is, there is my country.

※

*R*ather go to bed without dinner than to rise in debt.

※

*A*s we must account for every idle word, so must we account for every idle silence.

※

*D*o good to your friends to keep them, to your enemies to win them.

※

A great empire, like a great cake, is most easily diminished at the edges.

*T*o follow by faith alone is to follow blindly.

A pair of good ears will drain dry an hundred tongues.

*I*f you know how to spend less than you get, you have the philosopher's stone.

*W*ars are not paid for in wartime, the bill comes later.

*G*enius without education is like silver in the mine.

I guess I don't so much mind being old, as I mind being fat and old.

ॐ

O ne today is worth two tomorrows.

ॐ

I t is easier to prevent bad habits than to break them.

ॐ

H ide not your talents. They for use were made. What's a sundial in the shade?

ॐ

T he way to see by faith is to shut the eye of reason.

*E*xperience keeps a dear school, but fools will learn in no other.

*Y*ou can bear your own faults, and why not a fault in your wife?

*B*eauty and folly are old companions.

*S*avages we call them, because their manners differ from ours, which we think the perfection of civility; they think the same of theirs.

*H*e who falls in love with himself will have no rivals.

*M*any a man thinks he is buying pleasure, when he is really selling himself to it.

*L*aws too gentle are seldom obeyed; too severe, seldom executed.

*H*e that won't be counseled can't be helped.

*I*f a man empties his purse into his head, no one can take it from him.

*W*ho is rich? He that rejoices in his portion.

*N*ever take a wife till thou hast a house (and a fire) to
put her in.

※

*H*e that speaks much, is much mistaken.

※

*G*ames lubricate the body and the mind.

※

*I*f a man could have half of his wishes, he would double
his troubles.

※

*E*at to please thyself, but dress to please others.

*N*o nation was ever ruined by trade.

❧

*I*f you would know the value of money, go and try to borrow some.

❧

*A*pplause waits on success.

❧

*G*od works wonders now and then; behold a lawyer, an honest man.

❧

*I*f you desire many things, many things will seem few.

A cypher and humility make the other
figures and virtues of tenfold value.

*B*uy what thou hast no need of and ere long thou shalt sell thy necessities.

❧

*W*rite your injuries in dust, your benefits in marble.

❧

*T*he strictest law sometimes becomes the severest injustice.

❧

*H*unger is the best pickle.

❧

*I*n the affairs of this world, men are saved not by faith, but by the want of it.

*T*omorrow, every fault is to be amended; but that tomorrow never comes.

❧

*W*ho is rich? He that is content. Who is that? Nobody.

❧

*H*ear reason, or she'll make you feel her.

❧

*H*e does not possess wealth; it possesses him.

❧

*T*he absent are never without fault, nor the present without excuse.

The worst wheel of the cart makes the most noise.

When befriended, remember it; when you befriend,
forget it.

To lengthen thy life, lessen thy meals.

Remember that credit is money.

Since thou are not sure of a minute,
throw not away an hour.

*H*e that waits upon fortune, is never sure of a dinner.

❧

*T*he eye of the master will do more work than
both his hands.

❧

*W*ho had deceived thee so often as thyself?

❧

*H*e that composes himself is wiser than he that
composes a book.

❧

*I*t is much easier to suppress a first desire than to satisfy
those that follow.

*I*f you would have a faithful servant, and one that you like, serve yourself.

❧

*O*bserve all men, thyself most.

❧

*E*mploy thy time well, if thou meanest to gain leisure.

❧

*M*any foxes grow gray but few grow good.

❧

*W*here sense is wanting, everything is wanting.

The use of money is all the advantage there is in having it.

❧

He that's secure is not safe.

❧

Fatigue is the best pillow.

❧

Wealth is not his that has it, but his that enjoys it.

❧

Trouble springs from idleness, and grievous toil from needless ease.

*I*f everyone is thinking alike, then no one is thinking.

☙

*T*he art of acting consists in keeping people from
coughing.

☙

*I*ndustry need not wish.

☙

*T*he discontented man finds no easy chair.

☙

*N*ine men in ten are would-be suicides.

The first mistake in public business is the going into it.

❧

Early to bed and early to rise makes a man healthy, wealthy and wise.

❧

Mine is better than ours.

❧

Necessity never made a good bargain.

❧

Our necessities never equal our wants.

*T*ricks and treachery are the practice of fools that don't have brains enough to be honest.

*I*t is the working man who is the happy man. It is the idle man who is the miserable man.

*B*e at war with your vices, at peace with your neighbors, and let every new year find you a better man.

I wake up every morning at nine and grab for the morning paper. Then I look at the obituary page. If my name is not on it, I get up.

*H*ow few there are who have courage enough to own their faults, or resolution enough to mend them.

❧

*I*t takes many good deeds to build a good reputation, and only one bad one to lose it.

❧

*A*ll mankind is divided into three classes: those that are immovable, those that are movable, and those that move.

❧

*W*ithout continual growth and progress, such words as improvement, achievement, and success have no meaning.

*H*e that is of the opinion money will do everything may well be suspected of doing everything for money.

❦

*M*ost people return small favors, acknowledge medium ones and repay greater ones—with ingratitude.

❦

*Y*our net worth to the world is usually determined by what remains after your bad habits are subtracted from your good ones.

❦

*M*arriage is the most natural state of man, and the state in which you will find solid happiness.

*D*ost thou love life? Then do not squander time, for that is the stuff life is made of.

※

*I*f all printers were determined not to print anything till they were sure it would offend nobody, there would be very little printed.

※

I look upon death to be as necessary to our constitution as sleep. We shall rise refreshed in the morning.

※

I conceive that the great part of the miseries of mankind are brought upon them by false estimates they have made of the value of things.

*A*ll who think cannot but see there is a sanction like that of religion which binds us in partnership in the serious work of the world.

❧

*A*t twenty years of age the will reigns; at thirty, the wit; and at forty, the judgment.

❧

*I*t is the eye of other people that ruin us. If I were blind I would want, neither fine clothes, fine houses or fine furniture.

❧

*H*e that displays too often his wife and his wallet is in danger of having both of them borrowed.

*L*eisure is the time for doing something useful.
This leisure the diligent person will obtain
the lazy one never.

*T*here is no kind of dishonesty into which otherwise
good people more easily and frequently fall than that
of defrauding the government.

*I*f time be of all things the most precious, wasting time
must be the greatest prodigality.

*W*hen man and woman die, as poets sung, his heart's
the last part moves, her last, the tongue.

*A*nd whether you're an honest man, or whether you're a thief, depends on whose solicitor has given me my brief.

*H*uman felicity is produced not as much by great pieces of good fortune that seldom happen as by little advantages that occur every day.

*I*n general, mankind, since the improvement of cookery, eats twice as much as nature requires.

*H*e that has done you a kindness will be more ready to do you another, than he whom you yourself have obliged.

*F*ear not death for the sooner we die, the longer we shall be immortal

*I*n wine there is wisdom, in beer there is freedom,
　　in water there is bacteria.

❧

*J*ustice will not be served until those who are unaffected
　　are as outraged as those who are.

❧

*H*ow many observe Christ's birthday!
　　How few, His precepts!

❧

*N*ever ruin an apology with an excuse.

❧

*B*y failing to prepare, you are preparing to fail.

When you're testing to see how deep water is, never use two feet.

❧

A slip of the foot you may soon recover, but a slip of the tongue you may never get over.

❧

It is the first responsibility of every citizen to question authority.

❧

'Tis a great confidence in a friend to tell him your faults; greater to tell him his.

❧

The person who deserves most pity is a lonesome one on a rainy day who doesn't know how to read.

A house is not a home unless it contains food and fire for the mind as well as the body.

❧

*I*f you're going through hell, keep going.

❧

*T*rouble knocked at the door, but, hearing laughter, hurried away.

❧

*I*f Jack's in love, he's no judge of Jill's beauty.

❧

*D*o not anticipate trouble, or worry about what may never happen. Keep in the sunlight.

Changing countries or beds, cures neither a bad manager, nor a fever.

Happiness depends more on the inward disposition of mind than on outward circumstances.

To find out a girl's faults, praise her to her girlfriends.

Lighthouses are more helpful than churches.

When the well is dry, we know the worth of water.

Flesh eating is unprovoked murder.

*B*e civil to all; sociable to many; familiar with few;
friend to one; enemy to none.

❧

*W*hen the people find that they can vote themselves
money, that will herald the end of the republic.

❧

*S*ecurity without liberty is called prison.

❧

*W*hoever would overthrow the liberty of a nation
must begin by subduing the freeness of speech.

❧

*T*o be humble to superiors is a duty, to equals courtesy,
to inferiors nobleness.

*W*hile we may not be able to control all that happens to us, we can control what happens inside us.

❧

A brother may not be a friend, but a friend will always be a brother.

❧

*F*rom a child I was fond of reading, and all the little money that came into my hands was ever laid out in books.

❧

*B*elieve none of what you hear, and only half of what you see.

❧

*T*he problem with doing nothing is not knowing when you're finished.

*W*e do not stop playing because we grow old, we grow old because we stop playing!

ॐ

*A*n ounce of prevention is worth a pound of cure.

ॐ

*T*hose things that hurt, instruct.

ॐ

*L*ove your enemies, for they tell you your faults.

ॐ

A good example is the best sermon.

The only thing that is more expensive than education is ignorance.

৯৫

Eat to live, don't live to eat.

৯৫

Fools make feasts and wise men eat them.

৯৫

No one cares what you know until they know that you care!

৯৫

Women are books, and men the readers be.

*A*bsence sharpens love, presence strengthens it.

❧

*R*eading makes a full man, meditation a profound man, discourse a clear man.

❧

*Y*ou will find the key to success under the alarm clock.

❧

*F*ear God, and your enemies will fear you.

❧

A false friend and a shadow attend only while the sun shines.

*F*art for freedom, fart for liberty—and fart proudly.

*S*o convenient a thing to be a reasonable creature, since it enables one to find or make a reason for everything one has a mind to do.

A man convinced against his will is of the same opinion still.

*T*here cannot be good living where there is not good drinking.

*F*or every minute spent in organizing, an hour is earned.

*Y*ou can do anything you set your mind to.

A learned blockhead is a greater blockhead than an ignorant one.

*C*ritics are our friends, they show us our faults.

*B*lessed is he who expects nothing, for he shall never be disappointed.

*A*n apple a day keeps the doctor away.

*D*on't cry over spilled milk.

৯৫

*G*lass, China, and Reputation, are easily cracked, and never well mended.

৯৫

*W*rite to please yourself. When you write to please others, you end up pleasing no one.

৯৫

*J*oy is not in things, it is in us.

৯৫

*T*hinking aloud is a habit which is responsible for most of mankind's misery.

*H*aste makes waste.

༒

*W*ithout freedom of thought there can be no such thing as wisdom; and no such thing as public liberty, without freedom of speech.

༒

*G*enius is nothing but a greater aptitude for patience.

༒

*T*he securest place is a prison cell, but there is no liberty.

༒

*A*ll would live long, but none would be old.

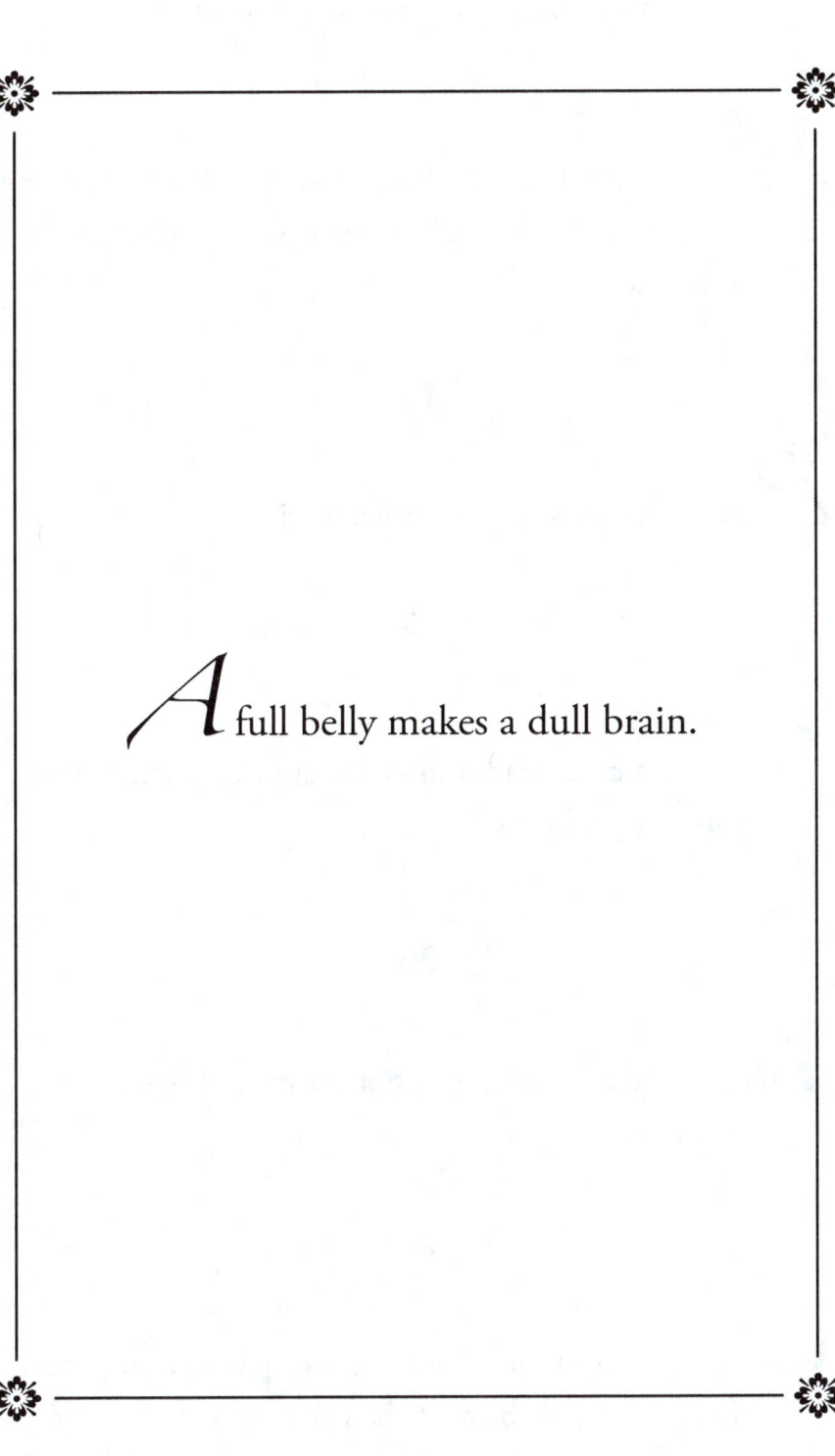

A full belly makes a dull brain.

*H*e that blows the coals in quarrels that he has nothing to do with, has no right to complain if the sparks fly in his face.

❧

*P*erhaps I'm too saucy or provoking?

❧

*I*f you have a bald head don't walk out in the sun because you will get burned.

❧

*T*o be proud of virtue, is to poison yourself with the antidote.

❧

*O*ld boys have their playthings as well as young ones; the difference is only in the price.

*S*erving God is doing good to man, but praying is
thought an easier service and therefore more
generally chosen.

❧

*N*othing ventured, nothing gained!

❧

*O*nly a virtuous people are capable of freedom. As
nations become corrupt and vicious, they have more
need of masters.

❧

*W*ould you live with ease, do what you ought, and
not what you please.

❧

*T*he purpose of money was to purchase one's freedom to
pursue that which is useful and interesting.

A countryman between two lawyers is like a fish between two cats.

T here are two ways to increase your wealth. Increase your means or decrease your wants. The best is to do both at the same time.

G od heals, and the doctor takes the fees.

A fter three days men grow weary, of a wench, a guest, and weather rainy.

S peak not but what may benefit others or yourself; avoid trifling conversation.

*L*et all your things have their places; let each part of
your business have its time.

❧

*R*esolve to perform what you ought; perform without
fail what you resolve.

❧

*E*at not to dullness; drink not to elevation.

❧

*L*ose no time; be always employed in something useful;
cut off all unnecessary actions.

❧

*T*he doorstep to the temple of wisdom is a knowledge of
our own ignorance.

To all apparent beauties blind, each blemish strikes an envious mind.

❧

Vicious actions are not hurtful because they are forbidden, but forbidden because they are hurtful.

❧

Be not sick too late, nor well too soon.

❧

Motivation is when your dreams put on work clothes.

❧

Look 'round the habitable world, how few know their own good, or, knowing it, pursue!

*G*reat beauty, great strength, and great riches are really and truly of no great use; a right heart exceeds all.

A friend in need is a friend indeed!

*L*iberality is not giving much, but giving wisely.

*W*hen nature gave us tears, she gave us leave to weep.

*R*eading was the only amusement I allowed myself.

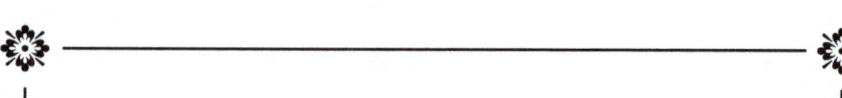

Are you angry that others disappoint you?
Remember you cannot depend
upon yourself.

*I*f all but myself were blind, I should want neither fine clothes, fine houses, nor fine furniture.

❧

*W*e choose the thoughts we allow ourselves to think, the passions we allow ourselves to feel, and the actions we allow ourselves to perform.

❧

*T*here never was a good knife made of bad steel.

❧

*R*ead much, but not many books.

❧

*O*riginality is the art of concealing your sources.

You have on hand those things that you need if you have but the wit and wisdom to use them.

I know not which lives more unnatural lives, obeying husbands, or commanding wives.

An old man in a house is a good sign.

Half-wits talk much, but say little.

Chess teaches foresight.

Let thy discontents be thy secrets; if the world knows them 'twill despise thee and increase them.

❧

We stand at the crossroads, each minute, each hour, each day, making choices.

❧

No gains without pains.

❧

Nothing is more fatal to health than an over care of it.

❧

To err is human, to repent divine; to persist devilish.

*C*onstant complaint is the poorest sort of pay for all the comforts we enjoy.

❧

*I*t is ill-manners to silence a fool and cruelty to let him go on.

❧

*W*ine makes daily living easier, less hurried with fewer tensions and more tolerance.

❧

*B*eware of the young doctor and the old barber.

❧

*T*he wise man draws more advantage from his enemies than the fool from his friends.

A truly great man will neither trample on a worm nor sneak to an emperor.

❧

V essels large may venture more, But little boats should keep near shore.

❧

D on't count your chickens before they are hatched.

❧

G ive me 26 lead soldiers and I will conquer the world.

❧

H e was so learned that he could name a horse in nine languages; so ignorant that he bought a cow to ride on.

A cheerful face is nearly as good for an invalid as healthy weather.

❧

*D*emocracy is two wolves and a lamb voting on what to have for lunch. Liberty is a well-armed lamb contesting the vote.

❧

*T*he cat in gloves catches no mice.

❧

*W*ish not so much to live long as to live well.

❧

*T*he rotten apple spoils his companions.

I am captivated more by dreams of the future then history of the past.

*F*inding myself to exist in the world, I believe I shall, in some shape or other, always exist.

*M*any a long dispute among divines may be thus abridged: It is so; it is not so. It is so; it is not so.

A rolling stone gathers no moss.

*I*t is hard for an empty sack to stand upright.

*T*art words make no friends; a spoonful of honey will catch more flies than a gallon of vinegar.

❧

*H*e that lies down with dogs shall rise up with fleas.

❧

*N*othing brings more pain than too much pleasure; nothing more bondage than too much liberty.

❧

*H*e that drinks his cider alone, let him catch his horse alone.

❧

I am in the prime of senility.

Work while it is called today for you know not how much you may be hindered tomorrow.

❧

He is ill clothed, who is bare of virtue.

❧

A ploughman on his legs is higher than a gentleman on his knees.

❧

What comfort can the vortices of Descartes give to a man who has whirlwinds in his bowels!

❧

Love your neighbor; yet don't pull down your hedge.

*T*he used key is always bright.

❧

*D*on't throw stones at your neighbors', if your own windows are glass.

❧

*B*e not disturbed at trifles, or at accidents common or unavoidable.

❧

*M*ake yourself sheep and the wolves will eat you.

❧

*T*here are three faithful friends in our life, an old wife, an old dog and ready money.

A real friend is one who always warns you.

*A*nd hence there is hardly such a thing to be found as an old woman who is not a good woman.

*I*f you eat one another, I don't see why we may not eat you.

*A*fter crosses and losses men grow humbler and wiser.

*W*hen women cease to be handsome, they study to be good.

*M*oderation . . . Avoid extremes,
forbear resenting.

*S*ilence . . . Avoid trifling conversation.

*T*ranquility . . . Be not disturbed at trifles.

*L*ove is blind. Friendship closes it eyes.

*B*ecause there is no hazard of children, which irregularly produced may be attended with much inconvenience.

*D*on't judge men's wealth or godliness by their Sunday appearance.

*I*f your head is made of wax, don't walk in the sun.

*T*hen plough deep, while sluggards sleep, and you shall have corn to sell and to keep.

*I*t isn't what you know that counts, it's what you think of in time.

*N*o European who has tasted savage life can afterwards bear to live in our societies.

A mob's a monster; heads enough but no brains.

*M*ake hay while the sun shines.

*I*gnorance leads men into a party, and shame keeps them from getting out again.

A life of leisure and a life of laziness are two different things. There will be sleeping enough in the grave.

❦

*P*roclaim not all thou knowest, all thou owest, all thou hast, nor all thou canst.

❦

*B*y my rambling digressions I perceive myself to be growing old.

❦

*I*n reality there is perhaps no one of our natural passions so hard to subdue as pride.

❦

*N*ot to oversee workmen is to leave them your purse open.

*D*iplomacy is seduction in another guise.

※

*W*e are not so sensible of the greatest health as of the least sickness.

※

*I*mitate Jesus and Socrates.

※

*D*id not strong connections draw me elsewhere, I believe Scotland would be the country I would choose to end my days in.

※

*I*f you would be wealthy, think of saving as well as getting.

*H*e that goes a-borrowing goes a-sorrowing.

*S*loth makes all things difficult, but industry,
all things easy.

*I*f you wouldst live long, live well, for folly and
wickedness shorten life.

*I*f you would persuade, you must appeal to interest rather
than intellect.

*S*earch others for their virtues, thyself for thy vices.

*C*reditors have better memories than debtors.

❧

*O*pportunity is the great bawd.

❧

'*T*is easy to see, hard to foresee.

❧

*W*hat is serving God? 'Tis doing good to man.

❧

*T*he poor have little, beggars none; the rich too much, enough not one.

He that speaks ill of the mare, will buy her.

Some are weatherwise, some are otherwise.

One good husband is worth two good wives; for the scarcer things are, the more they're valued.

A good lawyer, a bad neighbor.

Keep thy shop, and thy shop will keep thee.

The king's cheese is half wasted in parings; but no matter, 'tis made of the people's milk.

❧

When there's no law, there's no bread.

❧

He that hath a trade, hath an estate.

❧

What you seem to be, be really.

❧

There are more old drunkards than old doctors.

When knaves fall out, honest men get their goods.
When priests dispute, we come at the truth.

❧

Three good meals a day is bad living.

❧

Silence is not always a sign of wisdom, but babbling is
ever a folly.

❧

He that drinks fast, pays slow.

❧

Those who in quarrels interpose, must often wipe a
bloody nose.

The muses love the morning.

૨૬

He that would fish, must venture his bait.

૨૬

Drink does not drown care, but waters it, and makes it grow faster.

૨૬

The sleeping fox catches no poultry. Up! up!

૨૬

The church, the state, and the poor, are 3 daughters which we should maintain, but not portion off.

*T*hose who are feared are hated.

*I*t's common for men to give pretended reasons instead of one real one.

*T*here are no fools so troublesome as those that have wit.

*S*ell not virtue to purchase wealth, nor liberty to purchase power.

*S*udden power is apt to be insolent, sudden liberty saucy; that behaves best which has grown gradually.

Pride that dines on vanity, sups on contempt.

❧

Married in haste, we oft repent at leisure.

❧

Saying and doing, have quarreled and parted.

❧

Laws like to cobwebs catch small flies, great ones break thro' before your eyes.

❧

Success has ruined many a man.

*W*ink at small faults; remember thou hast great ones.

*I*n 200 years will people remember us as traitors or heroes? That is the question we must ask.

*B*eware of meat twice boiled, and an old foe reconciled.

*T*he most exquisite folly is made of wisdom spun too fine.

*G*reat modesty often hides great merit.

You cannot pluck roses without fear of thorns, nor enjoy a fair wife without danger of horns.

Men and melons are hard to know.

Idleness is the Dead Sea that swallows all virtues.

Take counsel in wine, but resolve afterwards in water.

A change of fortune hurts a wise man no more than a change of the moon.

*W*hen you're an anvil, hold you still; When you're a hammer, strike your fill.

❧

*S*he that paints her face, thinks of her tail.

❧

*I*f men are so wicked as we now see them with religion what would they be if without it?

❧

*L*et thy vices die before thee.

❧

*P*ride gets into the coach, and shame mounts behind.

*N*either a fortress nor a maidenhead will hold out long after they begin to parlay.

❧

*L*et all men know thee, but no man know thee thoroughly: men freely ford that see the shallows.

❧

A flatterer never seems absurd: the flattered always takes his word.

❧

*G*ive me yesterday's bread, this day's flesh, and last year's cider.

❧

*T*he Golden Age never was the present age.

*A*n ounce of wit that is bought,
is worth a pound that is taught.

*A*s nations become corrupt and vicious, they have more need of masters.

❧

*T*here have been as great souls unknown to fame as any of the most famous.

❧

*I*dleness and pride tax with a heavier hand than kings and parliaments.

❧

*D*on't overload gratitude; if you do, she'll kick.

❧

*H*e is a governor that governs his passions, and he is a servant that serves them.

*T*each your child to hold his tongue, he'll learn fast
enough to speak.

❧

*T*here is much difference between imitating a good man,
and counterfeiting him.

❧

*P*resumption first blinds a man, then sets him running.

❧

*G*reat talkers should be cropt, for they've no need
of ears.

❧

*M*en take more pains to mask than to mend.

*C*ut the wings of your hens and hopes, lest they lead you a-weary. Dance after them.

*F*riends are the true sceptres of princes.

*D*on't think to hunt two hares with one dog.

*T*he morning daylight appears plainer when you put out your candle.

*H*e's a fool that makes his doctor his heir.

*I*f evils come not, then our fears are vain: and if they do, fear but augments the pain.

❧

*V*ice knows she's ugly, so puts on her mask.

❧

*I*f you'd lose a troublesome visitor, lend him money.

❧

*T*he busy man has few idle visitors; to the boiling pot the flies come not.

❧

*N*one are deceived but they that confide.

*H*e that would have a short Lent, let him borrow money to be repaid at Easter.

❧

*L*ate children, early orphans.

❧

*H*e that scatters thorns, let him not go barefoot.

❧

*T*he proof of gold is fire; the proof of woman, gold, the proof of man, a woman.

❧

*T*he tongue offends, and the ears get the cuffing.

One mend-fault is worth two find-faults, but one find-fault is better than two make-faults.

❧

Innocence is its own defense.

❧

'Tis not a holiday that's not kept holy.

❧

An egg today is better than a hen tomorrow.

❧

Man's tongue is soft, and bone doth lack; yet a stroke therewith may break a man's back.

*B*eware of him that is slow to anger;
   he is angry for something,
      and will not be pleased for nothing.

*W*hen death puts out our flame, the snuff will tell, if we were wax, or tallow by the smell.

※

I think the best way of doing good to the poor, is not making them easy in poverty, but leading or driving them out of it.

※

*S*pare and have is better than spend and crave.

※

*D*eath takes no bribes.

※

*A*n ill wound, but not an ill name, may be healed.

*M*any would live by their wits, but break
for want of stock.

*V*irtue and happiness are mother and daughter.

A lie stands on one leg, truth on two.

*W*ealth and content are not always bed-fellows.

*N*othing dries sooner than a tear.

*T*ime eateth all things, could old poets say, The times are chang'd, our times drink all away.

æ

*T*he poor man must walk to get meat for his stomach, the rich man to get a stomach to his meat.

æ

*I*f you would have guests merry with your cheer, Be so yourself, or so at least appear.

æ

*B*lame-all and praise-all are two blockheads.

æ

A man in a passion rides a mad horse.

*L*ook before, or you'll find yourself behind.

৯৫

*M*any dishes many diseases, many medicines
 few cures.

৯৫

*T*ho' the mastiff be gentle, yet bite him not by the lip.

৯৫

*D*ifferent sects like different clocks, may be all near the
 matter, 'tho they don't quite agree.

৯৫

*F*or my own part, when I am employed in serving others,
 I do not look upon myself as conferring favours, but
 as paying debts.

The sting of a reproach, is the truth of it.

A modern wit is one of David's fools.

Freedom of speech is a principal pillar of a free government.

Work as if you were to live 100 years, pray as if you were to die tomorrow.

Doing an injury puts you below your enemy; revenging one makes you but even with him; forgiving it sets you above him.

*M*ost people dislike vanity in others whatever share they have of it themselves.

*B*eware the hobby that eats.

*H*istory will also afford frequent opportunities of showing the necessity of a public religion.

*I*t is easier to build two chimneys than to keep one in fuel.

*G*eese are but geese tho' we may think 'em swans.

*T*ruth will be truth tho' it sometimes prove mortifying and distasteful.

❧

*A*mbition has its disappointments to sour us, but never the good fortune to satisfy us.

❧

*M*ankind naturally and generally love to be flatter'd.

❧

*U*se no hurtful deceit. Think innocently and justly; and, if you speak, speak accordingly.

❧

*W*rong none, by doing injuries or omitting the benefits that are your duty.

*A*void extremes. Forbear resenting injuries so much as you think they deserve.

*T*olerate no uncleanliness in body, clothes, or habitation.

*T*he grand leap of the whale up the Fall of Niagara is esteemed, by all who have seen it, as one of the finest spectacles in nature.

*D*rinking beer doesn't make you fat, It makes you lean . . . against bars, tables, chairs, and poles.

*L*et thy maid servant be faithful, strong, and homely.

*A*t a great pennyworth,
pause a while.

*S*in is not hurtful because it is forbidden, but it is forbidden because it is hurtful.

❧

*P*overty often deprives a man of all spirit and virtue.

❧

*R*arely use venery but for health or offspring; never to dullness, weakness, or the injury of your own or another's peace or reputation.

❧

*T*he best thing to give to your enemy is forgiveness.

❧

*E*ducate your children to self-control.

We are all born ignorant, but one must work hard to remain stupid.

❧

Without justice, courage is weak.

❧

The nearest I can make it out, "Love your Enemies" means, "Hate your Friends."

❧

Despair ruins some, presumption many.

❧

You and I were long friends: you are now my enemy, and I am yours.

*M*en forget but never forgive. Women forgive but never forget.

∂⁺

*H*ear not ill of a friend, nor speak any of an enemy.

∂⁺

*D*eny self for self's sake.

∂⁺

'*T*is more noble to forgive, and more manly to despise, than to revenge an injury.

∂⁺

*T*he heart of a fool is in his mouth, but the mouth of a wise man is in his heart.

*A*t the working man's house hunger looks in but dares not enter.

❧

*W*ant of care does us more damage than want of knowledge.

❧

*D*oing your best means never stop trying.

❧

*A*n undutiful daughter will prove an unmanageable wife.

❧

*G*rowth means change and change involves risk, stepping from the known to the unknown.

*L*eisure is time for doing something useful; this leisure the diligent man will obtain, but the lazy man never.

❧

*T*he enemies you make by taking a decided stand generally have more respect for you than the friends you make by being on the fence.

❧

I have met the enemy, and it is the eyes of other people.

❧

A virtuous heretic shall be saved before a wicked Christian.

❧

*L*end money to an enemy, and thou will gain him, to a friend and thou will lose him.

*P*overty wants some things, luxury many things, avarice all things

❧

*M*oney never made a man happy yet, nor will it. The more a man has, the more he wants. Instead of filling a vacuum, it makes one.

❧

*F*riends may come and go, but enemies accumulate.

❧

*B*y working faithfully eight hours a day, you may get to be a boss and work twelve hours a day.

❧

*T*he pen is mightier than the sword.

*B*y diligence and patience, the mouse bit
in two the cable.

*I*f your riches are yours, why don't you take them with you to the other world?

❧

*W*hat maintains one vice would bring up two children.

❧

*H*andle your tools without mittens.

❧

*H*e has paid dear, very dear, for his whistle.

❧

*M*any have quarreled about religion that never practiced it.

*W*hoever feels pain in hearing a good character of his neighbor, will feel a pleasure in the reverse.

❧

*T*hose who love deeply never grow old; they may die of old age, but they die young.

❧

*A*nger warms the invention, but over heats the oven.

❧

A wise man will desire no more than what he may get justly, use soberly, distribute cheerfully, and leave contentedly.

❧

A benevolent man should allow a few faults in himself, to keep his friends in countenance.

*L*et honesty and industry be thy constant companions, and spend one penny less than thy clear gains.

❧

*P*ride breakfasted with plenty, dined with poverty, supped with infamy.

❧

*H*e's the best physician that knows the worthlessness of the most medicines.

❧

*T*o bear other people's afflictions, everyone has courage and enough to spare.

❧

A fat kitchen, a lean will.

'Tis against some men's principle to pay interest, and seems against others' interest to pay the principle.

Nothing gives an author so much pleasure as to find his works respectfully quoted by other learned authors.

Ere you consult your fancy, consult your purse.

Let the child's first lesson be obedience, and the second will be what thou wilt.

A little neglect may breed great mischief.

*M*any a one, for the sake of finery on the back, has gone
with a hungry belly, and half-starved their families.

❧

*N*one preaches better than the ant,
and she says nothing.

❧

*I*t is foolish to lay out money for the purchase
of repentance.

❧

*T*he best is the cheapest.

❧

*H*e that can take rest is greater than he that can
take cities.

*W*aste neither time nor money, but make the best use of both. Without industry and frugality, nothing will do, and with them everything.

❧

*S*queamish stomachs cannot eat without pickles.

❧

*R*ice is known to be one of the best sorts of food we have. Some whole provinces and even kingdoms are nourished by it.

❧

*B*e temperate in wine, in eating, girls, and sloth, or the gout will seize you and plague you both.

❧

*W*hat signifies knowing the names, if you know not the nature of things.

We must not in the course of public life expect immediate approbation and immediate grateful acknowledgment of our services.

❧

Rich widows are the only secondhand goods that sell at first-class prices.

❧

A plural legislature is as necessary to good government as a single executive.

❧

It is not enough that your legislature should be numerous; it should also be divided.

❧

If you do not hear reason she will rap you on the knuckles.

*A*n old young man, will be a young old man.

※

*W*e are more thoroughly an enlightened people, with
respect to our political interests, than perhaps any
other under heaven.

※

*T*hose disputing, contradicting, and confuting people are
generally unfortunate in their affairs.

※

A man may, if he knows not how to save as he gets,
keep his nose all his life to the grindstone, and die
not worth a grout at last.

※

*I*f you can't pay for a thing, don't buy it. If you can't get
paid for it, don't sell it.

*L*ying rides upon debt's back.

*S*ingularity in the right hath ruined many; happy those who are convinced of the general opinion.

*A*mong the numerous luxuries of the table . . . coffee may be considered as one of the most valuable.

*P*romises may fit the friends, but non-performance will turn them into enemies.

A light purse is a heavy curse.

*L*earn of the skillful; he that teaches himself, has a fool for his master.

*R*emember, that money is of the prolific, generating nature. Money can beget money, and its offspring can beget more, and so on.

*A*lways to suppose one's friends may be right till one finds them wrong, rather than to suppose them wrong till one finds them right.

*A*ll human situations have their inconveniences.

I am lord of myself, accountable to none.

*B*e studious in your profession,
     and you will be learned.

*B*e industrious and frugal,
     and you will be rich.

*B*e sober and temperate,
     and you will be healthy.

*B*e in general virtuous,
     and you will be happy.

*H*e that murders a crown, destroys all that it might have produced, even scores of pounds.

❧

*A*noint a villain and he'll stab you; stab him, and he'll anoint you.

❧

*B*ad commentators spoil the best of books.

❧

*B*e always ashamed to catch thyself idle.

❧

*H*unger never saw bad bread.

*I*f you would keep your secret from an enemy, tell it not to a friend.

❧

*C*lean your finger before you point at my spots.

❧

*C*heese and salty meat should be sparingly eaten.

❧

A soft tongue may strike hard.

❧

*N*othing but money is sweeter than honey.

The bell calls others to church, but itself never minds the sermon.

※

Watch the pennies and the dollars will take care of themselves.

※

Visits should be short, like a winter's day.

※

There are lazy minds as well as lazy bodies.

※

Moderation in all things—including moderation.

*W*e feel those of the present but neither see nor feel those of the future.

❧

*N*one but the well-bred man know how to confess a fault, or acknowledge himself in an error.

❧

*S*peak little, do much.

❧

*T*he sun of liberty is set; you must light up the candle of industry and economy.

❧

*T*o be intimate with a foolish friend, is like going to bed with a razor.

*F*ools need advice most, but wise men only are the better for it.

*N*o man's life, liberty or fortune is safe while our legislature is in session.

*I*t would be thought a hard government that should tax its people one tenth part.

A Bible and a newspaper in every house, a good school in every district.

*T*o be thrown upon one's own resources, is to be cast in the very lap of fortune.

*I*f you do what you should not, you must bear what you would not.

❧

I begin to be almost sorry I was born so soon, since I cannot have the happiness of knowing what will be known a hundred years hence.

❧

*H*e gives twice that gives soon, i.e., he will soon be called to give again.

❧

*I*t is wonderful how preposterously the affairs of the world are managed.

❧

*N*eglect kills injuries, revenge increases them.

I think vital religion has always suffered when orthodoxy is more regarded than virtue.

❧

*T*he scriptures assure me that at the last day we shall not be examined on what we thought but what we did.

❧

*H*e who shall introduce into public affairs the principles of Christianity, will revolutionize the world.

❧

*A*n innocent plowman is more worthy than a vicious prince.

❧

*W*ise men talk because they have something to say; fools talk because they have to say something.

The man who achieves makes many mistakes, but he never makes the biggest mistake of all—doing nothing.

❧

Gain may be temporary and uncertain; but ever while you live, expense is constant and certain.

❧

I believe opinions should be judged by their influences and effects.

❧

Anger and folly walk cheek by jowl.

❧

There was never a truly great man that was not at the same time truly virtuous.

*T*hose who govern do not generally like to take the trouble of considering and carrying into execution new projects.

⁂

I should have no objection to go over the same life from its beginning to the end.

⁂

*W*ho is powerful? He that governs his passions.

⁂

*I*t is a grand mistake to think of being great without goodness.

⁂

*W*ho is wise? He that learns from everyone.

*A*s sore places meet most rubs,
  proud folks meet most affronts.

*M*any estates are spent in the getting, since women for tea forsake spinning and knitting, and men for punch forsake hewing and splitting.

*I*t would not be altogether absurd if a man were to thank God for his vanity among the other comforts of life.

*A*varice and happiness never saw each other.

*D*eath takes both the weak and the strong.

*W*e are taxed twice as much by our idleness, three times as much by our pride, and four times as much by our folly.

I wish the Bald Eagle had not been chosen as the representative of our country; he is a bird of bad moral character.

❧

*H*ere comes the orator with his flood of words and drop of reason.

❧

*C*reditors are a superstitious sect; great observers of set days and times.

❧

*T*hree removes is as bad as a fire.

❧

*P*ainters have found it difficult to distinguish in their art a rising from a setting sun.

*E*very man among us reads, and is so easy in his circumstances as to have leisure for conversations of improvement.

❧

*T*here are no ugly loves nor handsome prisons.

❧

*A*t a great pennyworth, pause a while.

❧

*T*o be proud of knowledge is to be blind with light.

❧

*W*ise men . . . learn by others' harms, fools scarcely by their own.

*P*erhaps the history of the errors of mankind, all things considered, is more valuable and interesting than that of their discoveries.

❧

*H*istorians relate not so much what is done as what they would have believed.

❧

*M*an is a tool-making animal.

❧

*P*raise to the undeserving is severe satire.

❧

A poet is the mere wastepaper of mankind.

The greatest monarch on the proudest throne is obliged to sit upon his own arse.

❧

A lean award is better than a fat judgment.

❧

Since I cannot govern my own tongue, though within my own teeth, how can I hope to govern the tongue of others?

❧

There is nothing so absurd as knowledge spun too fine.

❧

If you want something done, ask a busy person.

*W*hen you speak to a man, look on his eyes; when he speaks to you, look on his mouth.

*P*ride is said to be the last vice a man gets clear of.

A child thinks 20 shillings and 20 years can never be spent.

*G*od gives all things to industry.

*N*othing preaches better than the act.

Folly and wickedness shorten life.

God will certainly reward virtue and punish vice, either here or hereafter.

The best investment is in the tools of one's own trade.

The noblest question in the world is: What good may I do in it?

Strange that a man who has wit enough to write a satire should have folly enough to publish it.

*H*e who multiplies riches, multiplies cares.

❧

*T*he great secret to succeeding in conversation is to admire little, to hear much.

❧

*C*offee invites cheerfulness without intoxication.

❧

I think that a young state, like a young virgin, should modestly stay at home.

❧

*N*ever pretend to wit.

Christians are directed to have faith in Christ, as the effectual means of obtaining the change they desire.

৵

Laziness travels so slowly that poverty soon overtakes him.

৵

The more a man has, the more he wants.

৵

Ill customs and bad advice are seldom forgotten.

৵

Virtue alone is sufficient to make a man great, glorious, and happy.

The soul of man is immortal and will be treated with justice in another life respecting its conduct in this.

※

On our idle days we are mutinous and quarrelsome.

※

The riches of a country are to be valued by the quantity of labor of its inhabitants.

※

Fraud and deceit are never in a hurry.

※

A nation that makes unjust war is only a great gang.

*I*f any man flatters me, I'll flatter him again, though he were my best friend.

A nod from a lord is a breakfast for a fool.

*S*ome of the domestic evils of drunkenness are houses without windows.

*I*f principle is good for anything, it is worth living up to.

*J*ustice is as strictly due between neighbor nations as between neighbor citizens.

*A*sk and have,
   is sometimes dear buying.

*I*f we can sleep without dreaming, it is well that painful dreams are avoided.

*I*n rivers and bad governments, the lightest things swim at the top.

*T*he heaviest debt is that of gratitude when 'tis not in our power to repay it.

*A*s for the tyrant, there are a million of us still engaged at snatching away his sceptre.

*C*harming women can true converts make; we love the precept for the teacher's sake.

*T*hree things a man is most likely to be cheated in; a horse, a wig and a wife.

෪

*W*hat we call time enough always proves little enough.

෪

*C*hristianity commands us to pass by injuries; policy, to let them pass by us.

෪

*H*ast thou virtue? Acquire also the graces and beauties of virtue.

෪

*I*ndustry pays debts while despair increaseth them.

The ancients tell us what is best, but we must learn of the moderns what is fittest.

❧

Dum vivimus vivamus (Let us live while we live)

❧

Laws without morals are in vain.

❧

A long life may not be good enough, but a good life is long enough.

❧

My hour is eight o'clock, though it is an infallible rule, "*Sanat, sanctificat, et ditat, surgere mane.*"

*P*ride: disguise it, struggle with it, beat it down, stifle it, mortify it as much as one pleases, it is still alive.

❧

*L*ife is rather a state of embryo; a preparation for life.

❧

*H*ave you something to do tomorrow; do it today.

❧

*I*t is the duty of mankind on all suitable occasions to acknowledge their dependence on the Divine Being.

❧

*F*reedom is not a gift bestowed upon us by other men, but a right that belongs to us by the laws of God and nature.

A man without ceremony has need of great merit
in its place.

※

*T*he good education of youth has been esteemed by wise
men in all ages, as the surest foundation of
the happiness.

※

*B*ad habits and vices of the mind being, like diseases of
the body, more easily prevented than cured.

※

*F*or I do not think that thanks and compliments, though
repeated weekly, can discharge our real obligations to
each other.

*B*y heaven we understand a state of happiness, infinite in degree, and eternal in duration.

*E*ven the mixed, imperfect pleasures we enjoy in this world, are rather from God's goodness than our merit.

*R*emember, Job suffered, and was afterwards prosperous.

*I*t is a common observation here that our cause is the cause of all mankind, and that we are fighting for their liberty in defending our own.

*T*hink how great a proportion of mankind consists of weak and ignorant men and women.

*I*ndustry and constant employment are great preservatives of the morals and virtue of a nation.

*T*he married state is, after all our jokes, the happiest, being conformable to our natures.

*L*et us, therefore, beware of being lulled in to a dangerous security; and of being enervated and impoverished by luxury.

I think all the heretics I have known have been
virtuous men.

T he expenses required to prevent a war, are much lighter
than those that will, if not prevented, be absolutely
necessary to maintain it.

S lavery is such an atrocious debasement of human
nature, that its very extirpation, may sometimes open
a source of serious evils.

I shall cheerfully consent to exchange my liberty
of abusing others for the privilege of not being
abused myself.

*M*y father convinced me that nothing was useful which was not honest.

*L*et the fair sex be assured that I shall always treat them
and their affairs with the utmost decency
and respect.

❧

*T*his respect of all . . . induced me to avoid all discourse
that might tend to lessen the good opinion another
might have of his own religion.

❧

A cold April, the barn will fill.

❧

I have experienced many instances of being obliged . . .
to change opinions even on important subjects.

❧

*H*umility . . . Imitate Jesus.

*G*ood wives and good plantations are made by good husbands.

❧

*H*ope and faith may be more firmly grounded upon charity than charity upon hope and faith.

❧

*V*irtue is not secure until its practice has become habitual.

❧

*N*othing is so likely to make a man's fortune as virtue.

❧

*W*ithout virtue man can have no happiness.

*C*ontrary habits must be broken, and good ones acquired and established.

❦

*L*et no pleasure tempt thee, no profit allure thee, and no ambition corrupt thee.

❦

*A*s to Jesus of Nazareth . . . I think the system of morals and his religion . . . is the best the world ever saw, or is likely to see.

❦

*W*ith industry and good management, [Americans] may very well supply themselves with all they want.

❦

*M*ost men, indeed, as well as most sects in religion, think themselves in possession of all truth.

*H*e who shall introduce into public affairs the principles of Christianity, will revolutionize the world.

❧

A fine genius in his own country, is a like gold in the mine.

❧

*N*o power, how great so ever, can force men to change their opinions.

❧

O powerful goodness! Bountiful Father! Merciful Guide! Increase in me that wisdom which discovers my truest interest.

*A*s all history informs us, there has been in every state and kingdom a constant kind of warfare between the governing and the governed.

❦

*P*eople will pay as freely to gratify one passion as another—their resentment as their pride.

❦

*A*ct uprightly, and despise calumny; dirt may stick to a mud wall, but not to polish'd marble.

❦

*T*here is scarce a king in a hundred who would not, if he could, follow the example of Pharaoh—get first all the people's money.

*T*here is a natural inclination in mankind to kingly government. It sometimes relieves them from aristocratic domination.

❧

*I*t is therefore that, the older I grow, the more apt I am to doubt my own judgment of others.

❧

*T*hey would rather have one tyrant than five hundred. It gives more of the appearance of equality among citizens; and that they like.

❧

A wicked hero will turn his back to an innocent coward.

*I*t may be imagined by some . . . that we can never find men to serve us in the executive department without paying them well.

*A*nd, indeed, in all cases of public service, the less the profit, the greater the honor.

I must be contented with the satisfaction of having delivered my opinion frankly and done my duty.

I am apprehensive, therefore—perhaps too apprehensive—that the government of the States may, in future times, end in a monarchy.

A little house well-filled,
    a little field well-tilled, and
    a little wife well-willed are great riches.

*I*t is therefore that the older I grow, the more apt I am
to doubt my own judgment, and to pay more
respect to the judgment of others.

❧

A full belly is the mother of all evil.

❧

*W*e indeed seem to feel our own want of political
wisdom, since we have been running about
in search of it.

❧

*D*anger is sauce for prayers.

❧

*W*hen men are employed, they are best contented.

A house without woman and firelight, is like a body without soul or sprite.

❧

Courage would fight, but discretion won't let him.

❧

There is no little enemy.

❧

All blood is alike ancient.

❧

All things are cheap to the saving, dear to the wasteful.

*B*e neither silly, nor cunning, but wise.

*H*e that spits against the wind, spits in his own face.

*M*ost miss opportunity because it shows up in overalls and looks like work.

*B*eware, beware! He'll cheat without scruple, who can without fear.

*T*he Colonies are not supposed to be within the realm; they have assemblies of their own.

*A*mbition often spends foolishly what avarice had wickedly collected.

❧

*T*he pleasures of this world are rather from God's goodness than our own merit.

❧

A hundred thieves cannot strip one naked man, especially if his skin's off.

❧

*T*he learned fool writes his nonsense in better language than the unlearned; but still 'tis nonsense.

❧

*H*e that hath no ill fortune will be troubled with good.

*A*noint a villain and he'll stab you; stab him, and he'll anoint you.

*B*ad commentators spoil the best of books.

*L*ittle strokes fell great oaks.

*A*pprove not of him that commends all you say.

*E*ach year one vicious habit rooted out, in time might make the worst man good throughout.

A quiet conscience sleeps in thunder.

*P*ay what you owe and you'll know what's your own.

I believe there is one Supreme most perfect being. . . .
I believe He is pleased and delights in the happiness
of those He has created.

*S*elf-denial is really the highest self-gratification.

*A*s charms are nonsense, nonsense is a charm.

I resolve to speak ill of no man.

❧

A ship under sail and a big-bellied woman, are the handsomest two things that can be seen common.

❧

T hey cannot force a man to take stamps who chooses to do without them. They will not find a rebellion; they may, indeed, make one.

❧

B argaining has neither friends nor relations.

❧

C hildren and princes will quarrel for trifles.

A good man is seldom uneasy, an ill one never easy.

ॐ

I also believe that without His concurring aid we shall succeed in this political building no better than the Builders of Babel.

ॐ

*B*ad gains are truly losses.

ॐ

*M*ost fools think they are only ignorant.

*F*ull of courtesy, full of craft.

❧

*A*nd if a sparrow cannot fall to the ground without His notice, is it probable that an empire can rise without His aid?

❧

*H*e may well win the race that runs by himself.

❧

A man is not completely born until he be dead.